Barely There

Barely There

Short Poems

Yahia Lababidi

RESOURCE *Publications* • Eugene, Oregon

BARELY THERE
Short Poems

Resource Publications
An Imprint of Wipf and Stock Publishers
199 W. 8th Ave., Suite 3
Eugene, OR 97401
www.wipfandstock.com

ISBN 13: 978-1-62564-279-0
Manufactured in the U.S.A.

This book is dedicated to my dear wife, Diana C. Restrepo,
for showing me that the ultimate work of art,
is who we are and what we do.

Contents

Contents

Contents

BREATH

Beneath the intricate network of noise
there's a still more persistent tapestry
woven of whispers, murmurs and chants

It's the heaving breath of the very earth
carrying along the prayer of all things:
trees, ants, stones, creeks and mountains alike

All giving silent thanks and remembrance
each moment, as a tug on a rosary bead
while we hurry past, heedless of the mysteries

And, yet, every secret *wants* to be told
every shy creature to approach and trust us
if we patiently listen, with all our senses.

EMBRACING, WE LET GO

Perhaps, we are negotiating
not just with one, but always two
(who share the same soil, it is true)
one who lives, another who is dying

A shift in balance begins to take place
once a love of silence is confessed
its roots run deep, its shade a world
and her fruits impossible to forget

From the first, we surrender something
and, gradually, consent to be emptied
seduced by so much soundless music
drunk and sated through lipless mouths

What use to name this silent master
preparing us for dying or the Divine
—I'm not sure there is a difference—
but know in embracing, we let go.

EXCHANGES

Don't grieve. Anything you lose comes round in another form. —Rumi

What unexpected turns our losses take
in winding their way back into our arms:

an absent lover returns as many others,
a nation forsaken in the shape of a new life;

poems might take the place of parents
and friends gone come back as a wife.

If Love were not always a step ahead
how would it ensure we kept up the chase?

Spirit

Bodies are like poems,
a fraction of their power
resides in their skin
The rest belongs to the spirit
that swims through them.

REACHING

Yes, my Other, this is how
I always recognize you
upward-reaching and glad
within wing's wind of a Great Song.

Two of Us

There is the wounded one
maimed, vicious and grasping
Then there's the Other
invincible and, at times,
lending a steadying hand.

ST. SEBASTIAN

Sometimes, he found it difficult
to dislodge the arrows
preferring to keep them there
reverberating in silence
along with his invisible wounds.

FOR RIMBAUD

Could it be that, from the start
the thing he sought, this demon-angel,
was always just outside the page

That, after swimming the length of the alphabet,
with fine gills and deranging senses, he created
an opening for others, but a trap for himself?

If so, then slipping through those watery bars
was imperative, a chastened mysticism—
and freedom to write in the air, to be human.

MEDITATION

Prayer is also anesthesia,
so that we might cut deeper
and clean out our wounds.

When in doubt, meditate
upon your ancient ache.

THE OPPOSITE OF VIRTUE

One might say, a vice is a vise
never mind if metal or moral,
it's basically the same device

with cunning moveable jaws
designed to fix us in place
and cheat us of a chance at grace

Impervious to all advice, habit
hotly whispers false reassurance
while tightening its iron grip

It takes no effort to slip into vice,
but virtue is trickier to stick to
like the back of a bucking bronco.

Misread Signs

False prophet, nightly heralding a man-made god
gilding the air with promise of revelation
a song, in truth, no less sweet for being counterfeit,
let us forgive the short-sighted visionary

Pity the poor bird its ill-timed enthusiasm,
its unholy lapse of judgment and misplaced hymn
having mistaken a common streetlamp
for the miracle of a rising sun.

DEFIANT MUSE

With myth and parable, the defiant muse
reminds us of the art of being present
and then, how to vanish without a trace.

TAUT

Between the real
and the Ideal,
rejecting the one
rejected by the Other.

Rack of extremes
the slightest touch
and I echo
awful music.

SINCE

I have lost my silences
I have lost my Voice …
peddling an Eternal currency
in life's bustling marketplace
irrepressible song springs up
and is strangled, unsung.

Thoughts hesitate
to leave cave
sensing ambush.

MYSTERY OF DOORS

Every jammed door has its trick
how much pressure to apply
where to push, just so, how deep
at what angle to jiggle, pull out

So, too, with the apparently
difficult doors of opportunity
that stubbornly balk at all rattling
yet suddenly yield at the key moment.

SPOKESPERSONS

The privilege
and fiendish challenge
of trying to be
one of Silence's
trusted spokespersons.

Ambassadors

Words need not be the opposite of silence,
they might be its ambassadors
Would that we could rescue the profundity,
and eloquence, of silence for speech.

Mystic, Misfit

Born exile,
homeless at last
tormenting ideal
having become
beckoning reality.

FANCIFUL CREATORS

What fanciful creators we are:
bestowing *shock absorbers* on cars
sprinkling *tenderizer* on meats
and stitching *wrinkle-resistant* shirts

Such wishful thinking, this
giving away what we desire.

ADVICE

A word of advice
for the ubiquitous:
every once in a while,
make yourself scarce
so, upon your return,
you might be missed.

GAZE

A loving gaze is
sun, water and soil
for a soul to grow.

UNENTITLED

I have not found the key to myself
the one that will get the high gates
to swing wide open, and the lights
to come on, at once

When not denied entrance entirely
I fumble in the dark and stumble
blindly, run into doors and walls
groping and hoping

I knock my head against false ceilings
and trip on traps I forgot to remember
then, start at the sight of my reflection
bumping into myselves.

Mortality

Youth is passing, mortality
no longer an abstraction

It's tucked like a secret
in the folds of our flesh
it's written in the open
of our shifting features

Not in complete sentences, yet
with telling punctuation marks

Once, our blood sufficed
as the stimulant of choice
hurtling through our veins,
singing indestructibility.

If . . . Then

If it were not for fear or habit
then there would be daily glimpses
of the indestructible world
and intimations of immortality.

EQUATIONS

It's easier to be fearless
when we remember
that we are deathless.

When beside yourself, blindfolded and bundled off
where all is winking confidences, suffused smiles
and a sense of imminent revelation
(a state as delineated as a planet)

try not to steal from this capital of riches
but cultivate organs of appreciation,
seek to acquire a taste for the return
and above all, remember the Way.

Truth in Advertising

Morning epiphany
in haiku-like purity:
only freshly squeezed
separation is natural
shake well to enjoy!
In fructose veritas.

DIETS

Imagination devours
everything it cannot see
Spirit is a fussy eater

Mind makes a scrap of feasts
and Desire a feast of scraps

Ego demands prime cut
meats and rich sweets
The rest is indigestion.

Dusk to Dawn

Dusk scuttles, quietly
like a crab
imperceptible as eternity

Dawn sands stand perforated
by bird footprints
in the shape of airplanes.

HIDE AND SEEK

The moon quickly hid behind clouds
when I stepped out to greet her

She knows I've not been faithful
and will not squander her Light.

The moon is back at my balcony
neither bashful, nor reproachful

She doesn't care who looks at her
she's full, now, of her own Beauty.

DESERT TRANCE

Under a whirling skirt of sky
streaming light and stars
groping for that tremendous hem,
gingerly over quicksand

As though transfixed beneath
some giant tongue and dissolving,
not the absence of sound
but the presence of silence

Under the ever watchful eye—
fearsome sun, forgiving moon—
bless the magnificent hand
all else is blasphemy, a lie.

Mountains

Old guards of the gods, elephantine
in girth and remembrance,
the imperishable memory
of the desert

School of inscrutable sphinxes
master storytellers sworn to secrecy,
pitiless witnesses of majestic grace
and menace.

I Saw My Face

I saw my face this morning
hovering at the base
of a coffee cup

eyes liquid black
and thirsting
lips parted as if

some great spoon
had stirred me to the depths
and left everything swirling.

Skin

Funny thing, skin
how it can make you feel
like you belong
to another or the world.

With its distinct instincts
memory and desire,
almost makes you wonder
who's wearing who?

EROS

Makes our eyes glisten
or lines of verse shine

Eros:

our last defense
against the dust.

KISSES

Two types of kisses,
and the choice is yours:
either with burning lips
that bind and blind,

or the lipless kind
always preparing us
to leave behind
a too-tight skin.

STRETCHES

I stand helpless before
the sensuality of stretches,
but get down on bended knee
for the spiritual variety.

Resume

Ah, the tragicomedy
of a spiritual asthmatic
straining for prophesy.

STAMINA

Hope is more patient
than fickle despair
and, so, outlasts it.

A Metaphor

Where ocean and shore greet,
a metaphor,
for where Spirit and body meet.

HOPE

Hope's not quite as it seems;
it's slimmer than you'd think
and less steady on its feet

Sometimes, it's out of breath
can hardly see ahead
and cries itself to sleep

It may not tell you all this
or the times it cheated death
but, if you knew it, you'd know
how Hope can keep a secret.

Morning

Every day, regardless
of the night's previous
sulks or arguments,

morning climbs into bed
breathless as a child
eager to play.

Sisyphus

You, brooding on boulder, shoulder
and impossible slope:
yield to crushing truths
relinquish aches and muscles, alike
relish the respite and commence, again.

Yield

Not by pushing
does one get ahead,
but by allowing
oneself to be pulled
by the constant
tug of all things.

LIBERATION

And, once you've arrived at the perimeters
of personality
that knot of contradictions, idiosyncrasies
called character

through the hall of mirrors
that comfort and distort

the liberation of undifferentiation
awaits the well-ventilated soul.

INCOMMUNICABLE

Shuddering certainty, where before
there was only intimation

Safeguarding her Secret
existence makes a mockery of words;
meaningless, they disperse
with a piercing glance

The belly of Being rumbles,
Eternity beckons.

WHAT IF

If he truly believed in angels
they would appear, I said in a dream
(of whom I spoke I can't recall)

Then I remember disintegrating
into hot tears as I realized
that I also spoke of myself

And in that wild, greedy moment
I challenged an angel to appear
as I cowered in a darkened closet

Full of longing and terror, I endured
the suspense of that great What If
—relieved the angel did not answer.

DESTINY

When anxious, Destiny gathers me in
with promises of otherworldly allure
outside of all specificity

In turn, I honor it in all things
as it follows me everywhere
with eyes dark and tender

Even in its night, I walk in light
in the dawn of understanding
and centered in its gravity.

CIRCUMSTANCES

The mind is full
of elephants and mice
scuffling in corridors

The air is dense
with stray spirits
swarming for soul

Heart like a spider's web—
misstep, and one is caught
carried away, helpless.

COLOMBIA

Here, in Medellin, what night lights—
like a resplendent necklace, glittering
against the bare throat of the mountains

Softly, coming in and out of focus
as though the mountains were breathing
between sharing a tender memory
of the city, with the valley and themselves.

The Poet

In the park this morning, a boy
bespectacled, gangly, impish grin
idly chasing a squirrel guarding an acorn;
both proceed in crouches and pounces.

Trailing behind them, a man
bespectacled, bearded, bemused
armed with a tell-tale pen and notebook
the poet eavesdrops on youth and life.

HARD DAYS

These are the hard days
like uncrackable nuts
break your teeth trying.

Faces turned heavenward
pitiful little satellites
transmitting intolerable Longing.

POET TRY

Verse versatile
yet word weary
Trust in longing
to sing itself.

Till the soil
until the soul
erupts into flower.

MASTER AND SERVANT

Rarely, having neglected his art
the man catches a glimpse of the artist

the cold, appraising gaze
that glint of an eye-tooth

better to turn away from the mirror
and best not to have a blade in hand.

ARTISTS

Whatever else artists may be
—monster, angel, battleground—
they are also tuning forks:
struck at every turn and
vibrating some hymn.

PEN PAL

He went to bed cradling a pen
his back turned to the woman
When he awoke, she was gone
and, in her place, a giant pen.

COORDINATES

One day, you will arrive
at the edge of your mind

and there you will find
that it is flat and thin

Only in leaping, definitively
will you know where you stand.

LOVE

Devoted to life of the mind,
he came late to love poetry
—through songs of adoration,
ecstasy and surrender—
addressed to the Divine.

EXPEDITION

After decades of exploration,
discovering I stand at the shore
of intellectual knowledge
before an infinite sea
of the esoteric.

OPTIONS

You can't bury pain
and not expect it
to grow roots.

But you can try
and tend tenderly
to its subtle fruits.

OVERHEARD

I have been lavishly gifted with a pain
as thick and rich as oil paint
By pushing it around the page
I have learned to make Art.

SURROGATES

Denied the balancing hand
of sane and loving parents
he ransacked libraries and worlds
emotionally, for a mother
intellectually, a father.

FEEDINGS

Attending to demons can be
a little like raising infants,
you simply cannot accept
every kind invitation

Sometimes, you must stay home
and feed the hungry things
heaping mouthfuls of your flesh,
till they finally fall asleep.

I-LASHES

Mind gnashing
for something substantial
to confidently sink
hungry teeth into

Heart lurching
searching for still
running waters
to cool hot hands in.

HOTHOUSE

I cannot bear
the perfumed air
of certain poets

where all is sweetness and verse
until someone dares to speak
without scenting their words, first.

Hunter and Hunted

Herding words, gathering world
spinning a wheel-shaped web
out of oneself, and waiting

To catch something of sustenance
wrap it in silk and ingest it
so that I might dream again.

SHORT ETERNITIES

... and when we soul–gaze
for short eternities it seems
her pupils dilate, vastly
become a universe
darkly gleaming—
to absorb you,
she says.

Dark Room

Awoke, with an unseen
reel of dream film
I'd found wandering

And, now, wondering
where does one develop
such unreal pictures?

DRYLANDS

Tell me, have you found a sea
deep enough to swim in
deep enough to drown in

waters to engage you
distract you, keep you
from crossing to the other shore?

Afterthought

And, when we pass, are we caught
in the pockets of afterlife
—the sorted and unsorted—

Or, do we continue slipping
through a fault in the lining
through the gaps in space?

LOVERS

What is a mystic
but one who swoons,
defenseless in the face of Beauty.

Egypt

You are the deep fissure in my sleep,
that hard reality underneath
a stack of soft-cushioning illusions.
Self-exiled, even after all these years,
I remain your ever-adoring captive

I register as inner tremors
—across oceans and continents—
the flap of your giant wing, struggling
to be free, and know I shall not rest until
your glorious metamorphosis is complete.

Kneeling in Stages

Twenty years ago, a mighty spirit
whispered to me and rearranged my days
Drink, it said, of solitude, taste of silence;
I did as told and it left me a writer

Now, it's back again with grander designs
to rewrite my soul or transform my being
Renounce, it insists, both word and world games
and I have no choice but to submit and bow.

Publication Credits

With gratitude to the fine editors who published these poems:

NPR, Tell Me More
Spirit
Reaching
Hunter and Hunted

Numéro Cinq
Exchanges
St. Sebastian
Pen Pal
Master and Servant

Berfrois
Embracing, We Let Go
Dark Room

Orbis
Truth in Advertising

Leviathan: Journal of Melville studies
Drylands

The Arab Review
Breath
Overheard

Delmarva Review
I Saw My Face

Publication Credits

Le Zaporogue
Mystery of Doors

The Monongahela Review
Unentitled

Generation Defining Itself – Anthology (volume 8)
Afterthought

Arts & Opinion
Morning
Liberation
The Poet

Mahmag World Literature
Circumstances
Colombia

Radius of Arab American Writers (RAWI)
Fanciful Creators

Islamic Writer's Alliance (IWA)
Desert Trance

www.ingramcontent.com/pod-product-compliance
Lightning Source LLC
LaVergne TN
LVHW021617080426
835510LV00019B/2619